Success Tweets

For Creating Positive Personal Impact

140 Bits of Common Sense Career Advice
All in 140 Characters or Less

BUD BILANICH
The Common Sense Guy

&

LYDIA RAMSEY

FRONT ROW PRESS

Front Row Press
191 University Boulevard, #414 • Denver, CO 80206 • 303.393.0446

This book is for Cathy, Bud's wife;
and Lauren and Linda, Lydia's daughters.

xoxoxoxoxoxoxoxoxoxoxoxoxoxoxoxoxoxoxoxoxoxo
xoxoxoxoxoxoxoxoxoxoxoxoxoxoxoxoxoxoxoxoxoxo
xoxoxoxoxoxoxoxoxoxoxoxoxoxoxoxoxoxoxoxoxoxo
xoxoxoxoxoxoxoxoxoxoxoxoxoxoxoxoxoxoxoxoxoxo
xoxoxoxoxoxoxoxoxoxoxoxoxoxoxoxoxoxoxoxoxoxo
xoxoxoxoxoxoxoxoxoxoxoxoxoxoxoxoxoxoxoxoxoxo
xoxoxoxoxoxoxoxoxoxoxoxoxoxoxoxoxoxoxoxoxoxo

That's 140 hugs and kisses…

Thanks to the three of you for your love and support.

A Note From
The Publisher

When *Success Tweets: 140 Bits of Common Sense Career Success Advice, All in 140 Characters or Less* was published in early 2010 my plan was that it would be the first in a series of tweets books helping people create the life and career success they want and deserve.

I published two more Success Tweets books in 2011: *Success Tweets for Finding a Job and Excelling in It*, coauthored by Billie Sucher and me; and *Success Tweets for Administrative Professionals,* written by me with input from Ketty Ortega and Chrissy Scivicque.

Success Tweets for Creating Positive Personal Impact is the fourth book in this series. It is a collaborative effort between Lydia Ramsey, author of *Manners That Sell*, and me. I hope you enjoy this little book and find it helpful as you go about creating the life and career success you want and deserve.

Bud Bilanich

Publisher, Front Row Press

Introduction

This is a career success book, containing 140 tweets. It will help you create the life and career success you want and deserve.

It gives you 140 bits of common sense life and career success advice, all in 140 characters or less.

It shows you how to create positive personal impact, an important skill for branding yourself as a polished professional.

Branding yourself as a polished professional is an important career success skill. This book will show you what to do and how to do it.

As with all of the *Success Tweets* books, you'll get the essentials with no fluff.

Your time is valuable. You don't want to waste it. That's why you get these 140 bits of advice

Twitter-style, in 140 characters or less.

Branding yourself as a polished professional is simple common sense. It's not hard, but you need to do it right.

In this book, career coaches Lydia Ramsey and Bud Bilanich will guide you on your journey to becoming known as a polished professional.

The tweets that follow are solid career advice on how to create positive personal impact — an increasingly important career success skill.

Each of the points above is less than 140 characters. See? You can communicate a lot of useful information in 140 characters or less.

Tweet books won't replace traditional books. But this little book is a handy reference guide for appearing polished and poised.

Enjoy this book. But remember, we want to

talk with you, not to you. Please follow @LydiaRamseyLive and @BudBilanich on Twitter.

Join the conversation. Please tweet about your thoughts on the ideas we present in this book.

Table of Contents

In General

IN GENERAL

1

Learn and use the basic rules of etiquette. Social faux pas might not ruin your career, but they certainly won't help it.

IN GENERAL

2

Be gracious, kind and engaging. Everybody likes to be around polite and mannerly people.

3

Always act like a lady or gentleman. It's not old-fashioned; it's smart business and leads to life and career success.

IN GENERAL

4

Be courteous. It costs you nothing and it can mean everything to someone else. It also helps in getting what you want.

5

It's great to know the rules, but the most important etiquette tip is to help other people feel comfortable.

Personal Branding

PERSONAL BRANDING

6

Stand and be known for something. Create and nurture your unique personal brand.

PERSONAL BRANDING

7

Build your personal brand by being consistent and constant. Make sure everything you do is on brand, consistently and constantly.

PERSONAL BRANDING

8

Your personal brand should be uniquely you, but built on integrity. Integrity is doing the right thing when no one is looking.

PERSONAL BRANDING

9

Build your brand by being visible. Volunteer for tough jobs. Brand yourself as someone who makes significant contributions.

PERSONAL BRANDING

10

Personal branding takes work. Do whatever it takes to make sure people will think of you in the way you want them to.

PERSONAL BRANDING

11

A good personal brand highlights your uniqueness. Be unconventional, break a few rules. But don't get too far out there.

PERSONAL BRANDING

12

Nurture your network. What your friends, colleagues and customers say about you is how others will think of you and your brand.

PERSONAL BRANDING

13

Say "thank you" often. You'll succeed, build a strong personal brand and leave a legacy of being a nice person.

Dressing For Success

DRESSING FOR SUCCESS

14

Demonstrate self-respect and respect for others in your attire. Be impeccable in your presentation of self.

DRESSING FOR SUCCESS

15

Be well-groomed and appropriate for every situation. Always dress one level up from what is expected. You'll stand out from the crowd.

DRESSING FOR SUCCESS

16

Observe successful people in your company. What do they wear? Dress like them and you won't go wrong.

DRESSING FOR SUCCESS

17

"Business" is the first and most important word in "business casual." Dress as if you're going to work, not a sporting event or club.

DRESSING FOR SUCCESS

18

The definition of business casual is to dress down one notch from business professional so you can't go from your suit and tie to your favorite old jeans and t-shirt.

DRESSING FOR SUCCESS

19

A man's most professional dress is a business suit with matching coat and trousers, accompanied by a blue or white shirt and solid tie.

DRESSING FOR SUCCESS

20

The most professional look for a business woman is a skirted suit. That means a knee-length skirt with a matching jacket.

DRESSING FOR SUCCESS

21

Pay attention to your shoes. Whether you do or not, others will. Keep them in good condition, polished not scuffed, and professional.

22

Pants' length matters in business. For both men and women, trousers should break gently at the top of your foot or shoe.

23

Men need to make sure that their shoes and belt match each other: both black or both brown. Both in good condition.

DRESSING FOR SUCCESS

24

Socks count. Be sure that yours match what you are wearing, either your shoes or your pants and definitely each other. No white socks.

DRESSING FOR SUCCESS

25

Keep your clothes in good condition. The rumpled, unpressed look can derail your career.

DRESSING FOR SUCCESS

26

At business social events, keep in mind that your attire still needs to look professional. Your clothing choices matter.

DRESSING FOR SUCCESS

27

Accessories make a difference. From handbags to laptop cases, watches to earrings, all need to be of good quality and conservative.

Business Meal Etiquette

BUSINESS MEAL ETIQUETTE

28

Do you have trouble remembering which is your bread-and-butter plate? Think of a BMW. Left to right, it's bread, meat and water.

BUSINESS MEAL ETIQUETTE

29

Flatware is used from the outside in. Start with the utensils to the far left or far right of your plate or bowl.

BUSINESS MEAL ETIQUETTE

30

The napkin goes into your lap after everyone is seated. It never goes back on the table until all are finished and rising from the table.

BUSINESS MEAL ETIQUETTE

31

Never begin eating until everyone at your table is served. If someone's meal is late and he or she suggests you begin, you may do so.

BUSINESS MEAL ETIQUETTE

32

Bread is broken, never cut. Tear off one small piece at a time. Biting into the entire roll at once is a major faux pas.

BUSINESS MEAL ETIQUETTE

33

The coffee cup remains upright on your saucer even if you don't care for coffee. Turn it over only if the server asks you to.

BUSINESS MEAL ETIQUETTE

34

The red wine glass is held by the bowl to keep the wine at room temperature. The white wine glass is held by the stem to keep it cool.

35

At the beginning of the meal, food such as bread is passed to the right. The waiter serves from the left so this helps avoid collisions.

BUSINESS MEAL ETIQUETTE

36

When hosting a business meal, make sure
that the server knows to bring you the
check to avoid any embarrassing or
awkward moments.

BUSINESS MEAL ETIQUETTE

37

The host decides when to discuss business over a meal. For a business lunch, this usually occurs as soon as the orders are placed.

BUSINESS MEAL ETIQUETTE

38

Business dinners are more social occasions where the focus is on building relationships rather than closing deals.

39

As a guest, order in the mid-price range on the menu. It is equally offensive to order the cheapest item as to select the most costly.

BUSINESS MEAL ETIQUETTE

40

Engage others in conversation at a business meal. Speak to the people seated to your left and your right. Never let someone sit alone and silent.

BUSINESS MEAL ETIQUETTE

41

Keep your breath fresh. Brush, or use the strips after meals and coffee. Don't chew gum. Ever. It makes you look like a cow.

Building Strong Relationships

BUILDING STRONG RELATIONSHIPS

42

Get genuinely interested in others. Help bring out the best in everyone you know. Others will gravitate to you.

BUILDING STRONG RELATIONSHIPS

43

Keep confidences and avoid gossip. Don't embarrass others by repeating what they share with you — even if it isn't in confidence.

BUILDING STRONG RELATIONSHIPS

44

Use every social interaction to build and strengthen relationships. Strong relationships help you create positive personal impact.

BUILDING STRONG RELATIONSHIPS

45

Everyone has something to offer. Never dismiss anyone out of hand. Take the time to learn about other people.

BUILDING STRONG RELATIONSHIPS

46

Get to know yourself. Use your self-knowledge to better understand and relate to others.

BUILDING STRONG RELATIONSHIPS

47

Pay it forward. Build relationships by giving with no expectation of return.

BUILDING STRONG RELATIONSHIPS

48

When meeting someone new ask yourself, "What can I do to help this person?" You'll build stronger relationships thinking this way.

BUILDING STRONG RELATIONSHIPS

49

There is no quid pro quo in effective relationships. Do for others without being asked or waiting for them to do for you.

BUILDING STRONG RELATIONSHIPS

50

Be happy to see others succeed. Use their success to motivate you to create your greater success.

BUILDING STRONG RELATIONSHIPS

51

Trust is the glue that holds relationships together. The more you trust others, the more they will trust you.

BUILDING STRONG RELATIONSHIPS

52

Become widely trusted. Deliver on what you say you'll do. If you can't meet a commitment, let the other person know right away.

BUILDING STRONG RELATIONSHIPS

53

Resolve conflict positively. Treat it as an opportunity to strengthen, not destroy, relationships you've worked hard to build.

BUILDING STRONG RELATIONSHIPS

54

Settle disputes and resolve differences quickly. Don't let them drag on. Engage the other person in meaningful dialogue.

BUILDING STRONG RELATIONSHIPS

55

Be a consensus builder. Focus on where you agree with others. It's easier to create agreement this way.

BUILDING STRONG RELATIONSHIPS

56

Be responsible for yourself. No one can "make you angry." Choose to act in a civil, constructive manner in tense situations.

BUILDING STRONG RELATIONSHIPS

57

Do your job. Give credit to others for doing theirs. Everyone likes to work with people who share the credit for a job well done.

BUILDING STRONG RELATIONSHIPS

58

We all make mistakes. Own up to yours. You'll become known as a straight shooter, honest with yourself and others.

BUILDING STRONG RELATIONSHIPS

59

Punctuality is a simple way to show courtesy and respect for others. It should be valued as the heart and soul of good business.

BUILDING STRONG RELATIONSHIPS

60

Savvy business people know that "RSVP" means to send a reply regardless of whether they plan to attend an event or not.

Networking Etiquette

NETWORKING ETIQUETTE

61

Make the most of networking events by arriving five minutes early. That gives you the opportunity to speak to people as they enter.

NETWORKING ETIQUETTE

62

Make it a point to work the room and speak to as many people as possible. Set a goal of how many people you want to connect with.

NETWORKING ETIQUETTE

63

Be yourself, as Mom told you. Don't put on airs to impress clients. They will see right through you and soon become former clients.

NETWORKING ETIQUETTE

64

When you meet someone at a networking function, make sure you remember and use his or her name. People love the sound of their name.

NETWORKING ETIQUETTE

65

Be warm, pleasant, gracious and sensitive
to the interpersonal needs and anxieties
of others at networking events.

NETWORKING ETIQUETTE

66

Speak from your heart. Show that you care about yourself and the person with whom you are in conversation.

NETWORKING ETIQUETTE

67

Demonstrate your understanding of others' points of view. Listen well; ask questions if you don't understand.

NETWORKING ETIQUETTE

68

Use the 2/3 – 1/3 rule in networking conversations. Listen two-thirds of the time; speak one-third of the time.

NETWORKING ETIQUETTE

69

Focus your complete attention on the person with whom you are speaking. Don't look for others with whom you want to connect.

NETWORKING ETIQUETTE

70

Look for common ground with people you meet at networking functions. Find out about them, their life, their passions.

NETWORKING ETIQUETTE

71

Never approach two people in conversation. You may be interrupting a private discussion. Find groups of three or more or someone alone.

72

Go prepared with conversation starters. Have at least three topics you can discuss if the conversation lags. Stick with safe subjects.

NETWORKING ETIQUETTE

73

Make sure you have an exit line in case you get stuck with one person. Offer your exit line after you have finished speaking.

NETWORKING ETIQUETTE

74

Follow up after the event. If you promised to call, pick up the phone the next day to arrange that meeting or lunch you suggested.

Business Cards

BUSINESS CARDS

75

Never leave your office without plenty of your business cards. There is nothing more unprofessional than not having them with you.

BUSINESS CARDS

76

Keep your cards in a business card case that protects them from wear and tear. A crumpled business card makes a poor impression.

BUSINESS CARDS

77

Know where your business cards are at all times. The person who has to go through a self body search to find them loses credibility.

BUSINESS CARDS

78

Hand them out with discretion. Doling them out in multiples of 12 says your cards are of little value.

BUSINESS CARDS

79

Give and receive cards with your right hand — the hand of discretion. This makes a big difference when doing business internationally.

BUSINESS CARDS

80

Give the card so the person who is receiving it can read it without having to turn it around.

BUSINESS CARDS

81

Always comment on a card you receive. Note the logo, the business name or other piece of information to place value on the card.

82

Keep your business cards up-to-date. When any information changes, run, don't walk, to your nearest printer for new cards.

BUSINESS CARDS

83

Don't write notes to yourself on someone else's business card during the exchange. Do that later out of sight.

BUSINESS CARDS

84

Don't be aggressive when handing out your business cards. Wait to be asked or request the other person's card first.

Email Etiquette

EMAIL ETIQUETTE

85

Email is now the dominant form of business communication. Be brief. If your message is lengthy, it will not be read.

86

To be appealing, your email message should be made up of short sentences, short paragraphs and lots of white space.

EMAIL ETIQUETTE

87

Make sure that your subject line is a summary of your message; that it aligns with the content and what the reader is expecting to see.

88

Limit your email to one topic. You'll find your results go up when you keep to a single subject. Create another email for another topic.

EMAIL ETIQUETTE

89

Email has no tone of voice or body language. Choose your words carefully so that your message will not be misunderstood.

EMAIL ETIQUETTE

90

Email is not for disagreements. Never argue in email. Walk down the hall or pick up the phone for sensitive discussions.

EMAIL ETIQUETTE

91

Use spell check, but remember to go beyond spell check. It only knows if the word is spelled correctly, not whether it is used correctly.

EMAIL ETIQUETTE

92

Email is not private, so write nothing in your message that you couldn't bear to see on a billboard on your way into work.

EMAIL ETIQUETTE

93

Watch those email threads that grow like tumbleweeds. Before you hit "reply," review the chain of messages and consider "delete."

Telephone Courtesy

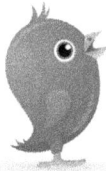

TELEPHONE COURTESY

94

Whether you are placing or answering a call, identify yourself immediately. The person on the other end should not have to ask your name.

TELEPHONE COURTESY

95

Ask permission before placing callers on hold and wait until you hear their answer before doing so.

TELEPHONE COURTESY

96

Before you transfer a call, make sure the person to whom you are sending your caller is available and has the correct information.

TELEPHONE COURTESY

97

Eating, drinking or chewing while talking on the phone is rude. The other person may not be able to see you, but will surely hear you.

TELEPHONE COURTESY

98

Give callers your full attention. It is obvious when people are multi-tasking while on the phone and it devalues the other person.

TELEPHONE COURTESY

99

Live people take precedence over phone calls. Continue in-person conversations rather than answering your cell phone.

TELEPHONE COURTESY

100

Cell phones should be kept off and out of sight when you are meeting with others. Just having yours on vibrate sends the wrong message.

Successful
Social Media

SUCCESSFUL SOCIAL MEDIA

101

The common sense rules of courtesy and civility that apply to in-person relationships are more important online.

SUCCESSFUL SOCIAL MEDIA

102

Social networks allow you to get known and help others. Give value and you will build a strong reputation online.

SUCCESSFUL SOCIAL MEDIA

103

Social networking is reciprocal. When you help people, they'll be more likely to remember you and return the favor.

104

Avoid being overly aggressive in social networking. If you are too persistent in pushing your agenda, you can damage your reputation.

SUCCESSFUL SOCIAL MEDIA

105

LinkedIn is the best social network for business professionals. Get active on it.

SUCCESSFUL SOCIAL MEDIA

106

For online profiles, use your real information and pictures. Your cat may be adorable, but that isn't the face you want to present to the world.

107

Post nothing you wouldn't want a would-be boss to see. Potential employers will Google you and make judgments based on what they find.

SUCCESSFUL SOCIAL MEDIA

108

Preserve your online reputation. Keep your promises when offering to facilitate a personal introduction or find a phone number.

SUCCESSFUL SOCIAL MEDIA

109

Use a different account or profile for your personal connections or websites. Remember, it is best not to mix business and pleasure.

SUCCESSFUL SOCIAL MEDIA

110

Offer real value, ideas and links to ideas that people can use to help their career or their business.

SUCCESSFUL SOCIAL MEDIA

111

Create screen names that reflect how you want to present yourself. Clever is good; cute is inappropriate. Your name is often the best choice.

112

Twitter is a great site to share information, meet new people and build your brand. Tweet items that have benefit for others.

SUCCESSFUL SOCIAL MEDIA

113

Retweet items that you think will be beneficial to others. You will gain more Twitter followers this way.

SUCCESSFUL SOCIAL MEDIA

114

Check out the people that befriend you or follow you. Others will judge you by the company you keep. Unwanted "friends" can cause harm.

SUCCESSFUL SOCIAL MEDIA

115

Compose your posts, updates or tweets in a word processing document before you post them, so you can check spelling and grammar.

SUCCESSFUL SOCIAL MEDIA

116

Remember there are no guarantees of privacy in social networks (even with settings). Anything can be cut, pasted, and sent.

SUCCESSFUL SOCIAL MEDIA

117

Never put anything on the Internet that you wouldn't want your boss, your coworkers or clients to see. It is not a secure place.

Meeting
Manners

MEETING MANNERS

118

If you are a first-timer in a group that meets regularly, ask where you should sit. Otherwise you risk taking someone's usual seat.

MEETING MANNERS

119

Don't try to look more important than you are. Constantly checking your watch or cell phone is distracting and rude to those around you.

MEETING MANNERS

120

Pay attention to your body language. If you are slumping, slouching and looking about the room, you are sending a negative message.

MEETING MANNERS

121

If you have a valid reason for leaving a meeting early, tell the speaker in advance to avoid any misunderstanding or appearing rude.

MEETING MANNERS

122

Prepare for the meeting. If an agenda is sent out in advance, read it, take a copy with you, and be ready to participate or take action.

123

Arrive on time. When you arrive late, you send a message that your time is more valuable than others or the meeting is not important.

MEETING MANNERS

124

Close your laptop, shut off your phone.
Respect the other people in the meeting
by giving them your full attention.

Introductions in Business

INTRODUCTIONS IN BUSINESS

125

When you encounter someone you don't know, immediately introduce yourself. Don't wait for someone else to do it for you.

INTRODUCTIONS IN BUSINESS

126

When you encounter someone you have not seen for a while, reintroduce yourself. Possibly that person has forgotten your name.

INTRODUCTIONS IN BUSINESS

127

When you can't remember someone's name, reintroduce yourself. Most likely he or she will respond in kind with their name.

INTRODUCTIONS IN BUSINESS

128

When making business introductions, introduce junior people to senior people. Start by saying the name of the senior person first.

INTRODUCTIONS IN BUSINESS

129

Never avoid an introduction because you can't remember someone's name. Confess your memory lapse and ask for the name.

INTRODUCTIONS IN BUSINESS

130

When meeting people, use their title (Mr., Mrs., or Ms.) until they give you permission to call them by their first name.

The Business Handshake

THE BUSINESS HANDSHAKE

131

People will judge you by your handshake. Yours should be firm, brief and inviting, not limp or bone-crushing.

THE BUSINESS HANDSHAKE

132

Men and women in business shake hands in the same manner. A man no longer needs to wait for the woman to extend her hand first.

THE BUSINESS HANDSHAKE

133

Always stand to shake hands. It shows courtesy and respect for the other person. By not standing, the business person loses credibility.

THE BUSINESS HANDSHAKE

134

If for some reason, such as an injury, you are unable to shake hands, always offer an apology and an explanation.

International Business

INTERNATIONAL BUSINESS

135

Be prepared before you travel. Read as much as you can and talk to other people about the countries where you will be doing business.

INTERNATIONAL BUSINESS

136

The handshake is the universal business greeting. While there are variations on the firmness and length, the right hand is always used.

INTERNATIONAL BUSINESS

137

Hugging and kissing are common greetings in business settings in parts of Europe and Asia. Do your homework and know what to expect.

INTERNATIONAL BUSINESS

138

Learn to bow. Most Asian cultures have adapted to the handshake. Show respect by learning their traditional customs as well.

INTERNATIONAL BUSINESS

139

Business attire is as important in other countries as it is here. Dress to the culture, which is often more conservative than U.S. dress.

INTERNATIONAL BUSINESS

140

Always send your host a hand-written thank you note. This is one tradition that will hopefully never change, no matter where you are.

ONE MORE THING

141

Because We Always Over Deliver, Here's One More Thing…

Knowing is not enough. Poised and polished professionals will read *and* act on this career advice. Be poised, polished and professional.

About Lydia and Bud

@LydiaRamseyLive, an international business etiquette expert helping you add the polish that builds profits: www.mannersthatsell.com

@BudBilanich, a life and career success coach helping you create the success you deserve. Let me help you succeed: www.BudBilanich.com

Success Tweets for Positive Personal Impact
makes a great gift!

Quantity discounts are available
from the publisher.

Call 303.393.0446 to inquire
about quantity pricing.